AMERICAN ODYSSEY

ALAN CATLIN

FUTURECYCLE PRESS
www.futurecycle.org

Library of Congress Control Number: 2016931957

Copyright © 2016 Alan Catlin
All Rights Reserved

Published by FutureCycle Press
Lexington, Kentucky, USA

ISBN 978-1-938853-96-8

For Valerie

Contents

"Teenagers," Brighton Beach, Coney Island...7
Mary Ellen Mark's Ward 81..8
Mary Ellen Mark's American Odyssey..10
Kelly Flores with Casper the Friendly Ghost, Halloween,
    HELP Shelter, South Bronx, N.Y., 1993..11
Tiny...12
Streetwise..13
After Watching the Documentary, "Streetwise" by Martin Ball,
    Cheryl McCall and Mary Ellen Mark..14
The Damm Family in Their Car...16
"James sleeping under the freeway," 1983..18
Mapplethorpe's Model (1980)..19
Mapplethorpe's Laurie..20
Mapplethorpe's Hand and Flower (1)...22
Mapplethorpe's Hand and Flower (2)...23
Mapplethorpe's Eileen 8/80...24
Mapplethorpe's Patti..26
Ralph Steadman's Orwell...27
Ralph Steadman's Dmitri Shostakovich...28
Ralph Steadman's Pepys..29
Ralph Steadman's The Brain of Dr. Hunter S. Thompson
    According to Gray's Anatomy...30
Ralph Steadman's Milosevic...31
Ralph Steadman's Macbeth...32
Ralph Steadman's Freud..33
Cosmic Dreamer Dreaming the Dream of the Universe.......................34
My Dream Date with Sylvia Plath..35
My Dream Date with Anne Sexton..36
My Dream Date with Diane Arbus...38
My Dream Date with Virginia Woolf..39
My Dream Date with the Brontë Sisters..42

My Dream Date with Frida 43
My Dream Date with Billie Holiday 44
Our Lady of the Striped Pajamas 45
Our Lady of the Kitchen Appliances 46
Our Lady of the Sub-Basement 47
Our Lady of Contraptions 48
Our Lady of the Trenches 49
Our Lady of Perpetual Longing 50
Samuel Beckett's Quadrant 1 & 2 as the Collapsing of the
   World Trade Center 52
The Assassination of John F. Kennedy as the Marathon
   Run Up Mt. Olympus 54
Judith with the Head of Holofernes as Original Sin 55
A Night of Serious Drinking as "Vertigo" 56
The "Russian Ark": History as Farce 57
Winged Victory as Wagner Heroine in a
   Wild Wild Wild West Show 58
After Viewing REQUIEM by Photographers
   Who Died in Vietnam and Indochina at the Eastman House,
   Rochester, N.Y., May 2001 59
Raising the Dead, REQUIEM Exhibit, Eastman House,
   Rochester, N.Y., May 2001 60
The Flower Arrangement at the Dead Photographer's Exhibit,
   REQUIEM, Eastman House, Rochester, N.Y., May 2001 61
Young Girl with Two Kittens, a Chicken and Her Father's Rifle,
   Vietnam, 1974 62
A Boy, a Dog and a Mortar 63
A Roadblock Marker along the Highway Outside Phnom Penh 64
Combat Elephants in Vietnam 65
R. Capa's Last Rolls of Film 66
Wandering in the Cage 67
The Girl in the Picture 68

"Teenagers," Brighton Beach, Coney Island

after photo by Mary Ellen Mark

They could be sisters
old enough to know what
trouble is, how to find it
and where, dressed for
the boardwalk or the beach:
cut low in the front bikini
tops, midriffs exposed,
cut-off short-shorts turned
down at the waist, exposing
more, signaling easy availability;
their "no messing around,
we mean business" faces
sexually astute, threatening
looks implying "come closer at
your own risk and, if you do,
better be ready to back up
and finish what you start."
They could be all of sixteen,
these girls, though fully
qualified as adults in certain
matters—that is, if experience
counts. They were never virgins.

Mary Ellen Mark's Ward 81

Once the inmates get used to
the idea of an intruder locked in
with the patients, the images she
creates are stills from a human
misery slide show, depict the horror
of what is left inside after the mind
has been removed. Poses are part
artifice, part grotesque parody of
what life might have been like before
the dark ages of perpetual bad-acid
flashbacks partially illuminated by
electroshock therapies, mind-altering
mood modifiers, personality stabilizers
like stun guns against rogue animals,
mortally wounded and suicidally self-
protective. Even the slight, young
woman, still retaining a quiet beauty,
no visible scars after multiple beatings
by her lover/husband wrapping bars
of soap in socks and applying the weapon
to her, mouth stuffed with a worn
flannel shirt still smelling of gasoline
and grease, a lifetime spent under vehicles
too broken to be fixed. After the beatings
he is repentant, swearing allegiances that
were vowed to be disobeyed, her skin
so cold to his touch, both inside and out,
he wonders where their love went.
Wonders why she takes knives, broken

glasses, hard edges of beer bottles to her
skin, watching the spilt blood as if it
belonged to someone else. When asked
why she felt compelled to mutilate such
immaculate skin she says, "I felt dead
inside, felt dirty and unworthy of life."
The initial pain was the first real thing
she had felt in years but even that seemed
unreal after awhile. When you see her
lying naked in the bath, wet hair clinging
to that small, heart-shaped, still-pretty face,
when you see her body, mostly unmarked,
desirable as the day she first felt love,
you can imagine her dressing to leave
this place, imagine her saying goodbye to
the girls she has lived with, felt closer to
than anyone else in her life, imagine first
kisses with the man waiting outside and
how, on Ward 81, they will not remove her
personal effects, not roll up her mattress
for the next one who will take her place,
knowing that while she may be leaving
today, in time she, too, will be back.

Mary Ellen Mark's American Odyssey

Memorial Day parade watchers, miniature
flag holder and the flags: circus tents and
the people who fill them, the twins separated
at birth, sword swallowers, tattoo artists and freaks
and the candy-colored clowns that watch them;
the shelter children, Halloween-costumed orphans
left behind on streets without dreams on city corners
in wicker baskets or in dumpsters like so much garbage
people close their eyes to in order not to see;
families in cars, in twenty-dollar motels for a night,
all six of them and the pets, filthy clothes washed
in sinks hung out to dry on shower stall rungs and
towel racks, six hours in occupancy and the room
is as totaled as the car left at the side of some
unnumbered road, already rusted and ravaged, seeming
as if it somehow had always been there; preteens
in wading pools sharing a smoke or dressed like ten-
dollar whores by the boardwalk; adolescent beauty queen
contestants, the winners and the losers, full-immersion
river Baptists, be-robed elevated train prophets and
their handlers working the aisles, donations on demand;
survivalist family training camps, children with guns
growing up to become armed teenagers in back alleys
a heartbeat from death, Charley McCarthy and Edgar
Bergen, talking heads backstage, the puppet master
and the illusionist; a child and his soon-to-be-dead
kitten, on Ward 81 and off, motherless and alone,
love and all the consequences, here, there, everywhere.

Kelly Flores with Casper the Friendly Ghost, Halloween, HELP Shelter, South Bronx, N.Y., 1993

after Mary Ellen Mark

In this impersonal place,
spare, undecorated like a
rent-by-the-hour (twenty
bucks an hour, clean sheets
and towels extra, maids always
at your service) room, the child
seems so small, smaller than
she actually is, perched on a
dresser table near the sound-off
picture-on TV, dressed as a
clown, a player in a children's opera,
a Punch and Judy play, already
a displaced person lacking clear
direction, looking puzzled, lost,
listening to whispered secrets,
encoded advice from Casper the
Friendly Ghost, emissary from
another, more forgiving world.

Tiny

She's of an age, thirteen going on
fourteen, where she's young enough
to dress up for Halloween in Salvation
Army rescue clothes: black hat and veil,
matching black velvet gloves and dress;
too old for door-to-door trick-or-treating
but available to receive what is offered.
Her way-beyond-innocent eyes suggest
she is comfortable with solicitation of any
kind once she learns it's all part of the job.
Perhaps the costume is a way of mourning
the childhood she never had, a sick joke
suggested by her significant other of
the moment or an older sister of the street,
part of her pimp's stable—the one who
instructed her in all the back-bedroom
black arts she'll ever need to know,
the same pimp who provided her with
the character-building thin scar on her chin
and who, later, when she can pass for maybe
sixteen, takes her for the first tattoo:
a demon bearing a pitchfork inscribed
on her right shoulder where her bra strap
would be if she had a reason to wear one.

Streetwise

Hanging by the graffiti wall: gang slogans,
dead kids walking, "I was here" magic
marker art, spray paint declarations against
The Man, the state, authority of any sort.
Instructions on where to hook up,
where the squats are, who's a narc and
who isn't. Teenaged hookers with their
who-can-afford-childcare kids.
Pimps like munchkins with knife fight
scars. The ones almost of age—too old
to be here, packing heat, 45s concealed
inside loose-fitting bomber jackets—wear
hats that say: BFD. Everyone on the street
knows that means *Big Fucking Deal*
or else they shouldn't be here or dead.
No one has any money, everyone smokes,
is hooked on something, everyone might
die tomorrow, but, today, this is the life,
this is really living.

After Watching the Documentary, "Streetwise" by Martin Ball, Cheryl McCall and Mary Ellen Mark

The elders, the ones they look up to,
the ones not currently in jail, are all
about eighteen with the reading skills
of a badly educated seven-year-old.
Up-and-coming street kids are all
working a grift: begging for change,
picking the pockets of the unwary and
the unwise, the ones too clueless
to know they are being had or are
about to be. Or rolling queers
outside of seedy nightclubs or
after rent-boy tricks. All of them
aspiring to be like the self-styled
playboy running a string of
underage girlfriends, young in years
but way beyond experienced.
Girls with backstories, moms on
the needle or drunk 24/7, no time
for needy kids or backup dads:
"My first step-dad was okay.
I actually kind of liked him.
The second one stuck it in before
I knew what it was.
The third one was worse.
Who can live in a home like that?"
They are an American version of Brazilian
Los Olvidados, the forgotten street kids,
too young to be tried as adults, too old
to be thought of as children.

They are all living a kind of *Requiem for
a Dream,* one that ends with a rusty-
needled arm turning black, or, dead
in custody, by their own hand,
all of them permanently scarred
or about to be. All these middle-teen
crazies, hanging out, dressed like their
younger sister with reindeer sweaters or
Tweety Bird T-shirts. Any number of them
marked "To Go" by the Green River Killer.
Which one will it be? Tiny or Denise or
Cheryl? Only time will tell.

The Damm Family in Their Car

after Mary Ellen Mark

All they owned was in the back seat
of the rusted-all-to-hell car with their
three kids and the dog. Mom still slim,
almost youthful, sexy in black form-fitting
tank top and too-tight jeans though her eyes
suggest another story, one that doesn't end well
due to frequent childbearing, always on the move
down a Route 66 of the body and the mind.
The passenger side of the car is wide open
at a rest stop for much-needed ventilation
and light. Dad's long, bare arms, defiled by
jailhouse tattoos and knife blade scars, is
wrapped around her neck in something like
a lover's hug, though loving isn't likely what
they will be doing in the car later in the night.
Their lives are ten thousand desert highway
miles ridden on the lam or looking for
work for a day or a week, though usually
the place they end up in is just another roadside
truck stop, bar or cafe they can raise hell in,
the kids locked in the car with their stuffed animals,
candy bar dinners and the dog. The car can't
pass a flashing neon beer sign as long as they
have some folding money to spend, as long as
he is behind the wheel, dragging her with him
whether she wants to go or not, knowing a couple
of cold ones down and she's the life of a honky-
tonk party. They never worry about the kids once

they are inside, those kids are too scared to stray,
curled up under filthy army surplus blankets,
a month of fast food containers, candy wrappers,
and junk-food bags illuminated by roadside
signs flashing off of their lean, pale, unwashed faces.

"James sleeping under the freeway," 1983

after Mary Ellen Mark

Homeless for years in his teens,
absent, plural parolee, father,
mother on a 24-hour drunk since
before he was born, Fetal Alcohol
Syndrome his legacy that lasts a
lifetime of sleeping raw, under
bridges, as the police and the weather
allow. Hanging with all the teenaged
hookers wearing the faces of someone
else's depression. Sharing stashes,
needles, whatever life on the street
provides. Turning tricks for steady
ready as rent boy or gigolo, it's all
the same to him in the end; protection
is what you pay the beat cop not to
notice whatever it is you are currently
doing. Has no idea what tomorrow will
bring. Barely knows what tomorrow is.

Mapplethorpe's Model (1980)

A shrewd interloper between old, lost worlds
and new ones few actually take the time
to see, keen eyes behind wide-rimmed glasses
containing life studies of all the indiscreet
pleasures of the middle class, Germany between
World Wars, a culture of self defeat, paranoia,
grim excesses exposed on park benches, sidewalk
cafes, outdoor concerts: the grossly overweight
and indulgent, petty bürgermeisters and hausfraus,
seamy undersides of everyday activities and hard-
life cafes becoming Coney Island matrons wallowing
in the surf, all of the seven beauties combined in one,
Dalí nightmare scene, giant shadows that dwarf
the men and women who cast them, these darkest
black and white Freudian Hitchcock sequences
becoming a tableau for a Laurie Anderson slow
tango with William S. Burroughs in living color,
a home of the brave gone berserk and all the crazy
Orson Welles interiors, camera angles, the refined
and the pure, society's finest staggering into hell
with half-filled martini glasses; after the happy hour is
over the fat ladies are silenced, the doorman is
the usher into dining areas for the dead, tips accepted,
double eagles for languorous, wandering, unseeing eyes
framed against a white brick wall, black shades drawn
to minimize unwanted light, reflections of immortality
in the merely mortal and the face that contains it all.

Mapplethorpe's Laurie

> *"Strange angels singing just for me*
> *Old stories they're haunting me*
> *This is nothing like I thought it would be"*
>
> —L. Anderson

What she is wearing defies
conventional standards of dress:
a too-large suit coat, padded
shoulders, button-down Oxford
cloth shirt fastened at the neck,
no tie needed for the semiformal
occasion of appearing onstage
or in the studio where no one
in Chuck Taylor sneakers fears
to tread. Only the top half of
her body is revealed, hair short
and wild, almost spiky, probably
dyed some unnatural color easily
highlighted by overhead spots,
staged lighting. She seems oddly
composed, pensive, features soft
and feminine belying easy assumptions
on androgyny, unusual humoresques
of past poses taken upside down,
tied by the ankles, dangling over
the Coney Island boardwalk with her
partner, Lou Reed, nearby, out for
a walk on some wild-sided afternoon
in Brooklyn or, at rest, as a strange

angel, her white hand resting beside her face, pure and perfect as a sculpted blessed virgin's hand, her heart-shaped face unadorned, unmade up, pale and beautiful against a black back drop.

Mapplethorpe's Hand and Flower (1)

The image is all about simplicity:
a contradiction in terms,

two objects in opposition,
carefully arranged and juxtaposed:

a hothouse orchid and a man's
clenched fist, anxiety and grief;

the longer they are observed,
the more similar they become.

Mapplethorpe's Hand and Flower (2)

The hand that held the flower,
held the whip, held an orchid,

a calla lily, an arrangement of
tulips, held fading roses in black

and white, others in bloom, in
color, held a gun in self-portraits,

made himself a woman in others,
smiling and in multiple disguises,

was a smear in the mirror, a smudge
on the wall; beauty and sadness,

disguised as a shock of the new.

Mapplethorpe's Eileen 8/80

Close up, the portrait could be
a yearbook photo, some kind of
postgraduate, looking back at
how it was: stoned and crazy
yet, somehow, in-control nightmare.
Or, maybe, a mug shot, if she
had time to actually pose, and
a whole series of takes to choose
from, for that all-important *Wanted*
poster anyone could look at in
the Post Office, waiting in line for
forever stamps or to ask stupid questions.
As if this were the kind of picture that
could advance your career, whatever that
was this week, or, more immediately,
to lay out lines of coke on, or hits of speed,
something no good Catholic girl would do;
living just this side of Jim Carroll's
The Basketball Diaries. Her look, and his,
like that of a pale horse, pale rider bearing
a death's-head with a crucifix to keep the vampires
temporarily at bay. Or maybe it was that snide
she-male-with-an-attitude look of an
androgynous party girl—half Patti Smith,
half Brian Jones—that captured you.
Made you sense she was some kind of
doomed rock star on the make,
wannabe poets getting off the way they did

on Jim Morrison, who might have been her:
separated-at-birth twin, before he became
a bloated lush. Or maybe, just maybe,
she had the look of a latent Man in the
White Suit: slightly wasted, but totally cool
and above it all, an alien being who
fell to earth, the one who worked in a jazz club
and lived in the basement of the Chelsea,
helping Jesus make a Satan's brew of moonshine
and blacklight mushrooms to sell
to the worm people who live under rocks,
only surfacing after dark, their tinted pupils
brushed by fire, all the better to see inside you.

Mapplethorpe's Patti

The walls she leaned against,
pale and white, serious as a
Picasso clown, a sideshow
siren, hair a mess, disheveled
after nights sleeping raw and
crazy, images wild on the page
and in her eyes, so vivid a camera
cannot capture what is inside,
the pictures she draws on the unseen
walls between them and how he
was rapt, in bondage to them
and all the pain he brought to
bear on the wounds, to the soft
flowers on black velvet, orchids
and calla lilies, and how night
unveiled their lives a layer at
a time, she a Salome receding,
he an Orpheus looking back into
the shadows, her shadows, his.

Ralph Steadman's Orwell

To shoot an elephant, first you
must experience fever dreams,
visions of lives lost in Asian
jungles, self-portraits ravished
by malarial fevers, a body at war
with itself, swollen limbs, a malaise
of the tongue, the marrow, the bones,
the brain returning to former lives
spent down and out in Paris and London,
squalid as a refugee from an animal farm,
pen, taking tea with wild boars, pigs,
sipping a Ceylonese brew, trying to
stave off the end, hate weeks, group-
think, them becoming us, a deathbed
confession, marriage in a Year of the Rat,
inauspicious as hell.

Ralph Steadman's Dmitri Shostakovich

The rift in Stalin's brain
is a symphonic line of musical
notes, an allegro moderato,
Dmitri S. in chains known to
Uncle Joe as a mere composer
of incidental music, movie scores,
though Dmitri's daily life remained
a well-monitored house of pain,
100 Days That Shook the World
forever flickering in his buckshot
eyes, scores savagely jump-cut
to keep him from a firing squad,
one strong quartet away from KGB
killers, a silent garrote; notations
in his score book written in blood.

Ralph Steadman's Pepys

"It was a sad noise
to hear our bell...."
inscribed in the artist's
calligraphic hand as Pepys,
the bold Colossus astride
the Thames, writing in his
diary, seeing through taxidermic
eyes; the tolling of the bells
a call to worship or the warning
of tumbrel drivers about to
pass, calling out for the dead
and dying, those Black Plague
years their work was never done,
London dusk a suttee fog, corpses
afire, the Bridge and slums as well.

Ralph Steadman's The Brain of Dr. Hunter S. Thompson According to Gray's Anatomy

The body is pure Steadman,
stripped of skin to reveal
the skeletal structure: vertebrae
and bone, elongated neck a perch
for the brain to rest on at the moment
of impact of mind-altering substances,
designer drugs and bonded bourbon,
volatile as chemical reactions: bursting
cranial sacs, separating brain matter
from frontal lobe, exploding hemispheres
a mass of severed body parts: hands and
arms and eyes, signature cigarette holder
still intact, filtered butt drooping, still
burning, ten years before a pistol to
the mouth made the imagined drawing real.

Ralph Steadman's Milosevic

His neck is elongated to giraffe length,
stretched like his illustrations of Alice's
red queen, extra flesh for the ruler's head
to avoid all the offal, decapitations he
has demanded; though, here, in Yugoslavia,
the bodies are all buried in unmarked graves
to be excavated as killing fields, forensic
evidence of a reign of terror even the dictator
cannot bring himself to consider, soiled as
he is dressed in pinstriped suit now a butcher's
apron covered in human gore and blood,
a vital organ in the lapel where a decorative
flower should be.

Ralph Steadman's Macbeth

It's after the nuclear war and
there's nothing left but one
barely mobile man stricken by
radiation sickness, stumbling
the last scorched acres of a killing
zone, a burnt orange sky at his
back, a broken cup in one hand
for scooping tainted water from
blood-tainted pools, a broken spear
in the other for impaling black birds
of prey pried loose from primordial
caves by a reckless savaging of the earth,
warrior face, a rubber mask melting
from bones so brittle they too shall
soon return to the dust all things
are made of.

Ralph Steadman's Freud

The sleeping man's head is
a bust, a fully featured
rock on a post, an impediment
to be climbed on by ant-like
creatures, weremen exploring
nasal cavities, ears, crawling
inside, dangling from eyebrows,
lids, entangled in beard, scruffy
hair, these human lice scuttling
about, exploring, poking about,
falling off rounded edges,
falling like insects, dreaming
Freud's head.

Cosmic Dreamer Dreaming the Dream of the Universe

Here the sculpted man twisted into
fetal knots, roughage removed
from imperfect stone, an occluded
vein hammered into submission,
chiseled until the hardest places
are like sleep running as ice melt
will when exposed to direct light or
a ripple of reflected moonlight
hardened into fingers cradling still-
forming embryos of dream becoming
that penultimate place where white noise is
filtered through raw cavities of rain
gradually assuming shapes that blacken
an endless waste of stillborn night;
all those sickening hours before dawn
neighborhood outlaws are compelled to
assemble shooting stars for the next wave
of temperature inversions, of self-
containment within hard glass globes
fraught by artificial weathering—
a man is a mean object here, created
only to be scorned, known only by
the acid rain that settles in the hollow
crevices, the empty sockets of his eyes.

My Dream Date with Sylvia Plath

"The music is too depressing,"
she says, "like something they
might play in the morning room
at MacLean's." The music is probably
by Beethoven but it sounds like Bach
to me. "Everything sounds like Bach
to you." She says, as if we were old
friends, as if we hadn't just met,
as if she could read my mind.
"Come on, let's go somewhere more private.
Maybe smoke us a cigarette." I don't
smoke but I always carry matches just
in case. You never know.
She says, "Here will do just fine."
I have no idea how we ended up in this
dark room, am about to strike a match
when she pulls me to her like a banshee in heat,
forcing her tongue between my lips,
"I know you want me. I can see all the way
inside you." I return her kiss, my energy
as strong as hers, or so I think, until she bites
me on the lips, drawing blood.
I say, "What did you do that for?"
"It's good to feel love and pain at the same time,"
she says, drawing aside the heavy drapes
of the morning room. Outside, bare winter
trees in the snow.

My Dream Date with Anne Sexton

In the poetry workshop
the white-haired man read
"Lycidas," the original, and his
corrections, the improved new
version, the one he swore was
infinitely superior to Milton's,
his normally deep voice turning
shrill as he spoke. "Your home-
work assignment is to rewrite
the fairy tale of your choice.
Class meets again next Monday,
as usual." Though everyone knew
it never would. After class Anne
and I went to the movies, shared
a cocktail shaker of extra-dry
Schenley's martinis, watched
with horrified fascination the opening
sequence of the latest Bond thriller,
thinking, later, the best thing about it
was McCartney singing, "Live and
let die! Live and let die!" over and
over, like a mantra, or some kind
of twisted dirge. Afterwards Anne
said, "I think I'll do the Brothers Grimm."
"Which one?" I asked.
"Both of them, preferably at the same time."
"But they're dead."
"It was a joke. Their fairy tales. Do them
as if they were an Alfred Hitchcock movie."

"Which movie?"

"Lifeboat."

I thought about being cast adrift.
About how it would feel to be absolutely
alone, abandoned by God. About all that
awful rowing.

My Dream Date with Diane Arbus

The place of our meeting decided well
in advance, after dark, in a theater on
42nd Street. The feature we will see,
"Freaks." I am the man too large for the room
I am confined in, and she, the lady in the wheelchair
wearing the fairy princess Halloween mask,
a pinwheel braided into her fright wig,
a magic flute hanging from a leather
strap around her neck she will blow
as I wheel her through the stalls,
down the long sloping aisles, entreating
the triplets and the twins to throw their sweets
into the wide-open trick-or-treat bag held
on her lap. The movie is not the black and white
"Freaks" set in a traveling carnival, starring midgets
and dwarves, pinheads and hydros, but the one
where all the actors are people from real life,
wearing paper faces cut from pages of
the daily news, all of them frozen in stilled lives,
enacting crimes of the century: imperialist wars
of occupation, assassinations and atrocities,
ritual torture and extreme rendition;
the starkest of them all, a boy in short pants
holding a hand grenade, pin pulled, his face
contorted, anticipating what happens after
the momentary pain.

My Dream Date with Virginia Woolf

Whatever outrageous comment I made must
have amused her. I thought I saw the suggestion
of a smile on her face, unless it was a trick of
the fading late-afternoon light. I was more
than a little stoned, half-drunk, no doubt, as well,
or *droned*, as my friend used to say, or *strunk*,
depending upon which high was in ascendance.
Whatever it was, I wouldn't have approached her
at all, unless I was one or the other, or both.
She had a well-earned reputation as the ice queen
on campus, dressed down to avoid anything
like feminine. Or anything for that matter.
I expect if you looked up "androgynous" in a
Pictionary, she'd be there as example number one.
Actually, the more I drank, the more I babbled,
filling the gaps in our one-sided conversation
with nonsense, the more attractive she seemed to me,
not at all like the two-bagged lady everyone made her
out to be. One bag, for sure, nothing was going to
change that, but I was willing to take the chance
that if her bag fell off at a crucial moment during
sex that her look wouldn't turn me to stone,
so I was willing to foreswear wearing mine.
That I was even willing to entertain such a ridiculous
thought was a clear indication of how far gone I was,
even for a student-faculty mixer, the only reason to go
was free watered-down whiskey sours and bad jug wine.
We shared a few upper-level Lit courses, and there was

no doubt she knew her shit and she wasn't showy about it
either. I suppose it was the combination of such
self-assured brilliance, and not caring about it,
that had made her more interesting to me than anyone
else I had encountered in nearly four years of
undistinguished academic achievements. Not that I
couldn't have done better if I chose to. Showing up
wasted for a final in my first survey course was a
less-than-inspired idea, and it was reflected in my grade.
It was just that kind of inspiration that had put me
on this talking jag I couldn't stop, even if wanted to.
Deep inside, I began to wonder what the hell was that
pot laced with, speed or what, but it was too late now
to unsmoke it or to put a stopper in my mouth.
Something I said, or was saying, must have touched
her in a bizarre way, something even she couldn't
put a name to. Most young women would either
have slapped my ass silly by now, or gone to the little
girls' room and never come back. But there Ginny
stood, almost smiling at me, waiting for what came next.
Or that's what I thought. I'm my own worst critic.
Always have been. Maybe she was waiting for me to implode,
or launch into orbit, or spontaneously combust, or something.
Who knows? Later on, I was almost tempted to read one
of her books to find out what she really thought about, but
I was never able to get past page three of any of them.
I don't remember which ones I tried; they all seemed
equally opaque to me. At some point, I must have
asked her if she wanted to, you know, like, get it on.
I can't recall her saying no, exactly, or what happened
after a certain point in that evening. I do recall waking

up around four the next afternoon, covered in mud,
with my pants around my knees and no sign of a woman,
Virginia or anyone else. Looking back, I'd hate to think I caused
her pain. That was never my intention. That kind of stuff just
happened. I was young and didn't know any better.
I'd like to think she knew that. I heard they found her
drowned with stones in her pocket. Man, that's just so weird.

My Dream Date with the Brontë Sisters

> *"The sheep know where they are,*
> *Browsing in their dirty-wool clouds,*
> *Gray as weather."*
>
> —*Sylvia Plath, "Wuthering Heights"*

In The Perfumed Garden, out front
of the three-chord-progression band
and in-another-dimension drummer, they
were the Three Weird Sisters, one-hit
wonders doing club gigs where the patrons
sat on the bar, stood on wobbly tables,
made mosh pit madness look like meat
grinders on legs with steel-tipped boots,
wore their bleached-blond hair buzz-cut
short, their dyed-green waxed Mohawk
wave-tall, their flock of seagulls pink fluff
acting like the screaming banshees on speed
they were, in tight leather minis, torn mesh
stockings, tank tops two sizes too small,
body art by Hokusai of New Jersey:
tsunami waves with burned-out ghetto
scenes, wild women with black flag decals
sewn beneath their chests. No one can
hear them over the band. No one understands
a word that they say.

My Dream Date with Frida

As the shadow gets ready to fall,
all the exotic birds of her mind
perch in primeval trees, on shoulders
sloped by pain, become the avian
part of a circulatory system exposed,
chest cavity split for easy viewing,
myna beaks where the heart should be.
Every thought she speaks has a bird in
the sentence, a feather for a weight
that tips the justice scales of her brain
from one side to the other, knocks
the axis from its place, fanning
a polar reverse; anything that was
up is now down, anything that was
rooted floats free. Even the paint she
uses to depict mirror images of herself
is now ruined, soiled by birds so tainted
with disease, their songs are the only
images that survive. Even clamped to
her bed, at the end, her birds surround
the place where she lies, burning the sheets
with their claws, summoning the smoke
that eludes their blind eyes, the way red
coals turn from ember to ash and back again
when the wind is right. When she cries out
for the loves of her life to save her from
the encroachment of night, strange birds
answer in an uncommon language only
they can understand.

My Dream Date with Billie Holiday

Lady Day sings the blues in an
open-all-night-club as the Resurrection
Jazz Band takes the stage to play their
tall black flutes, reeds stained by eternal
flames, rusty valves soldered to their
frames, impossible to move,
toy pianos and kiddie drums
too undersized to play, tin horn bent
and bored by plumber's snakes, router tips
still dangling from a well-chewed spout,
crude painting on the dented shaft.
The headless jazzmen are all dressed in
identical red suits, furious fists clenched
in the burnt sienna air amid a choking
wedge of flame. Lady Day strokes the blues,
the reds, the yellows, the white hearts
out of our ever-loving night, high on death
and tea bag dreams, her voice a razor blade
and we, in this open-all-night-club, are the skin.

Our Lady of the Striped Pajamas

This is the way the world ends:
within concentric circles of barbed
wire fencing patrolled by packs of
starving dogs inside the mined perimeter,
their trainers and sharpshooters watching
from elevated guideposts, smoking cigarettes
and scanning the grounds with floodlights,
emergency flares nearby just in case
the unlikely occurs: that those locked inside
could somehow escape, that some lady in
striped pajamas could show them the way
out, provide a path to the promised land
and somehow take them there instead of
leading them to their places in the courtyard
where the camp band plays Messiaen,
half the orchestra missing, most of the music
as well, on those unchanging, airless, no-hope
afternoons, before the sirens signal to those
assembled that all is clear.

Our Lady of the Kitchen Appliances

has razored out all the center
pages of the *New Joy of Cooking,*
from vegetables to game, and sewn in
the text of a *New Joy of Sex,*
listening to Dropkick Murphys as she
hand-mashes potatoes, muddles fruit,
adds spice to stuffing, strips layers
from a leg of lamb, rubbing the bare
flesh with herbs, spiking with garlic,
preparing a feast she can't wait to
shove inside the oven; boils extra water
until the kitchen is like a steam bath,
clothes clinging to her sweating body,
finally hot enough, she can really
begin to cook.

Our Lady of the Sub-Basement

Beneath diaphanous cloth is
the statue of the Savior,
right hand partially raised as
if to offer supplication, the other
held slightly above the head,
a prop for draping curtains,
three fingers upraised,
one each for separate aspects
of the Divine Trinity. An icon
such as this, so splendidly
carved, hand-painted, buffed
to appear so overtly holy
no one could mistake its intent.
No matter its origin or what
the statue represents, a better
resting place is deserved than
this cellar dwelling with gray
switch plate, grime-stained
by oily fingers, workman's gloves,
hands that provide illumination.
Perhaps this statue is not of
the Right Holy One but of a lesser
angel as Our Lady of the Sub-
Basement, Holy Mother of the
Elevator Shaft, Blessed Saint of
the Stock Room, her function
neglected for so long as to be
completely forgotten, part of
the general chaos, discarded furniture,
in transit to nowhere, junk and debris.

Our Lady of Contraptions

from the book of lesser saints, with apologies to Gray Jacobik

stands guard over kitchen
junk drawers
overflowing with parts

of dead appliances
one-handled can openers
damp matches

candles without wicks
stretched out of round blender seals
used-to-death twist ties

all the stuff that may
once have had functional
use and may yet

again if the unthinkable
comes true.

She is the forgotten sister
of St. Jude and is represented
by a kind of widget

constructed of used popsicle sticks
tufts of shed hair
of several deceased cats

and Christmas tree bubble lights
that no longer work.

Our Lady of the Trenches

traverses No Man's Land
at night carrying a Red
Cross flag through the mud,
through rolled barbed wire,
shell pits and mustard gas
clouds, as if she were some kind
of Florence Nightingale risen
from the dead, her nursing
uniform soiled and tattered,
her medical kit a bag of dirty
tricks and unrolled bandages,
her haggard face, unnaturally
pale skin, highlit by artillery
rounds flash-firing the murky
sky, her boots caked by all
manner of viscera, gone-putrid
skin of soldier boys, guard dogs
and mules of the dread instruments
of war; her face at first light
the last thing they see.

Our Lady of Perpetual Longing

sits in a low, three-legged stool
at the subway station of last resorts
holding a wooden bowl
outstretched with one hand, or
maybe she is sitting with the bowl
balanced on her lap, on the folds
of her many garments worn for
warmth in all seasons, her possibly
blind eyes hidden behind thick
black lenses, hair tied back and
covered by a tight-fitting snood,
face of indeterminate age revealing
nothing, as the money is offered
and received; the bills she periodically
removes, adding to her stash secreted
amid the clothing, occasionally adjusting
sound levels on her boom box in
accordance with time-of-the-day
traffic, most favored selections of
Palestrina, Hildegard von Bingen,
Gregorian chants, working her way
to the modern age, to the requiems
by the masters: Cherubini, Verdi,
Hector B., his Te Deum the clearest
expression of all that has been lost
and may never be replaced, at odds
with they who travel here, paying their
way, her music a kind of cacophony

echoing throughout the underground
while the voice of God is being
evoked for those who will listen and
those who will not.

Samuel Beckett's Quadrant 1 & 2 as the Collapsing of the World Trade Center

after reading Quan Barry

Four forms dressed in monks' robes are standing on two
>   separate metal quadrants, on two separate stages,
>   simultaneously in two separate theaters.

One stage is filmed in black and white and the other in color.
It doesn't matter which stage is filmed in color or which one
>   is filmed in black and white.

The colors of the robes: red, blue, green and yellow.
The figures are mute, sexless, and their heads are bowed, their
>   arms crossed and held close to their chests, hidden
>   within long, draping sleeves.

When the play filmed in color is acted live, the stage is lit from
>   above with soft shades, light coloring, nothing harsh or
>   jarring, nothing obnoxious or offensive to the eyes.

When filmed in black and white and acted live, the stage is
>   lit in plain white spots, soft lights making the coloring
>   more like shades and shadows than actual light.

The actors remain throughout the play as they are first seen,
>   never moving, never changing their position, never
>   acknowledging the existence of an audience watching,
>   waiting, expecting.

At some point music is heard, softly at first then more loudly until
>   it becomes uncomfortably loud.

It is a strange music, unlike any music ever heard in a theater as
>   an accompaniment to a stage presentation or anything else,
>   an instrumentation involving synthesizers, electrified pianos
>   and harpsichords, air raid sirens, insistent percussives provided
>   by solo drums repeating, one after the other:
>   on kettles, snares, tympani

and an occasional anvil strike
followed by an unexpected rain of ash, partially burnt papers,
> computer printouts, particle boards, pieces of insulation,
> asbestos ceiling tiles, all matter of unidentifiable debris
> softly floating down,

floating from everywhere, floating from nowhere.

Eight days after the destruction of the twin towers, Laurie Anderson's
> *Live at Town Hall, NYC* is taped as she sings, "O Superman—
> "here come the planes—"

The Assassination of John F. Kennedy as the Marathon Run Up Mt. Olympus

after reading Quan Barry and with apologies to J. G. Ballard

We've seen the pictures hundreds of times by now whether
    we cared to see them or not:
the originals of the motorcade in black and white followed
    by the bizarre shooting live of presumptive assassin
    Lee Harvey Oswald.
The unforgettable processional afterwards: the cortege, the banging
    of the drum slowly, John John's loyal salute.
And in color: the Zapruder tapes slowed down frame by frame
    on that warm, clear November Dallas day: Jack's bare
    head, Jackie's hat, Governor Connelly and his wife
    waving to the crowd, Jack's head exploding, blooming
    like some time-lapsed flower bursting open, smoke rising
    on the grassy knoll—
smoke rising like fog on Olympus wreathing the hidden peak and all
    that might dwell there.
26.2 miles of running steadily uphill over brutal, rocky terrain
    in summer's dreadful heart-stopping heat, the goal less
    and less realistic, less visible with each step upward,
    steps that bring you higher but no closer to the gods.

Judith with the Head of Holofernes as Original Sin

after reading Quan Barry

What could be more distressing than a sit-down dinner
    for eight and no main course?
The man late from his errand to provide, to retrieve
    the stipulated meal, arriving hours late, half-
    smashed after close encounters with others of
    his kind, the errand long ago forgotten.
An unexpected vision of the Virgin is detected in
    arrangements of cheeses, crackers and sliced
    breads further disrupting the disastrous meal.
Exasperated, Judith can no longer abide, hoists recently
    sharpened-for-carving knife, oblivious of the
    inevitable staining, ruination of her hostess gown,
    attacks the wayward man.
This Holofernes surprised, relaxing in his den with a
    fresh flagon of wine, has no reflexes, no time
    to react.
Once his head has been deftly removed, Judith and her
    handmaiden arrange it on a silver serving platter
    to present to the guests instead of the expected
    boar's head.
They were his guests, after all, and they are all agog,
    shocked by the grisly scene.
Who among them would take the garnishing apple left
    on the side of the platter and place it in their
    host's gaping mouth?

A Night of Serious Drinking as "Vertigo"

after reading Quan Barry

All the imbibers, the refugees are emancipated from
    the complete works of Vincent van Gogh:
the absinthe drinkers, potato eaters, self-portraits
    with and without ears,
all the close, musty rooms without adequate heat,
    poorly drawn fires, smoke filtering from long,
    clay pipes, loosely rolled tobacco and the tightly packed,
exhaustion apparent in all the worn faces, the downtrodden
    and the bedeviled, the unforgiving and the damned
    pounding down their
libation of choice on a night of serious drinking: the green
    fairy, essence of wormwood, conveyances of
    deep dreaming while awake, mortal stasis while
    breathing, metempsychoses in a bell-shaped glass.
Once paralysis is made liquid, bodily functions require
    a superhuman exercise of the will simply to consider
    locomotion;
standing upright becomes the purest form of vertigo there is.

The "Russian Ark": History as Farce

after reading Quan Barry

All of Russian History evoked in terms of Art,
    the streaming consciousness of hand-held
    camera free-floating through a walking,
    waking dream.
The real and the fictional as characters in an
    elaborate drama of light and dark as played
    by living exhibits extracted from the Hermitage
    walls; no time or room for errors, second
    takes on this whirlwind run-through.
No time for rewrites of the unseemly death of Catherine
    the Great, the exploits of that Russian giant
    among men, Peter the Great, nor of Alexander's
    deluded visions, fanatical love of all things god.
The Russian Ark of History as a wild roller coaster
    ride into a dark Siberian night:
Asylums that were not asylums but prison camps.
    Cancer wards.
    Gulags.
    Leper colonies.
    The pogroms.
All ignored.

First you are in the official photos.
Then you are not.

Winged Victory as Wagner Heroine in a Wild Wild Wild West Show

Even dressed in full plated armor, war weapon at
    the ready for action in one hand, forged metal
    shield in the other, she is primed for a Texas
    Two Step,
songs by Johnny Cash—"Love is a burning thing
        And it makes a fiery ring.
        Bound by wild desire..."—
lays down a perimeter of gasoline on the ground
    around her wounded man, taken down in
    a dueling pistols match with ATF agents
    during a personal shootout at the OK Corral,
lights a stick match on her teeth, watches as the black
    smoke rises against a red sky,
clouds shaped like flying horses with wings tipped
    by flame
as they descend, as these pale new riders of a purple
    sage wield lancers and swords,
power saws and stump removers, heading toward
    the Tree of Life, near the downed man and his lover,
lying, dying together, by a fetid inland sea,
the shore clotted with refuse, hot dog wrappers, McDonald's
    discards, old boots and spent condoms, tires and
    rubber rafts,
remnants of cookouts and barbeques, beer cans and
    bloodshed,
where the end of the world begins.

After Viewing REQUIEM by Photographers Who Died in Vietnam and Indochina at the Eastman House, Rochester, N.Y., May 2001

The dead are levitated in Vietnam,
made airborne to safe havens in Huey
holds, ripe for body bags and long trips
home, coffins swathed in stars and stripes.
The dead are piled beneath tank turrets,
blown away in Claymore mine explosions,
dropped down by artillery shells
or simply vaporized, brought back to earth
trapped in chopper holds, on assignment,
caught in volleys of ground to air, neutralized,
summarized in last film rolls, f-stopped forever.
The dead walk the line through jungle
thickets, engage in three-day pitched
battles never once sighting the enemy,
or ford monsoon-thickened rivers, just
two hands holding a weapon above
the current, visible. Apprehended at
checkpoints, the dead are questioned
and detained, never to be seen again,
or interrogated in bamboo forests,
gunshots signaling the death of family
members, comrades, just out of focus.
The dead are sometimes hung upside down
over low fires, heads grazing the flames,
or are killed outright, their heads severed
and placed on poles as a constant reminder:
the dead do not reveal secrets.
Everyone is dead in Vietnam.

Raising the Dead, REQUIEM Exhibit, Eastman House, Rochester, N.Y., May 2001

The dead are rising, spread-eagled
in mid-air, trussed to thick ropes,
grappling hooks beneath hovering craft.
A watchful eye imagines a *mise en scène*;
the unreality of a slain paratrooper on the rise,
resurrected without will time and time
again, jungle shadows blackening his
impossible face unmarked by battle,
puzzled by momentary, fragmentary
shocks of recognitioning, then this unnatural
levitation. This is no Lazarus robbed
from the grave, no Christ-like figure,
though his pose as dangling man floating
might suggest it. He is merely a dead man
trapped in an emulsion of dank humid air,
fragrant as cordite, odorous as a residue
of napalm stirred by chopper blades.

The Flower Arrangement at the Dead Photographer's Exhibit, REQUIEM, Eastman House, Rochester, N.Y., May 2001

What music could accompany this exhibit?
Twenty years of carnage begun, continued,
memorialized as an ongoing funeral of an age,
attended in silence by the curious, the involved,
the mourners; as a gift of remembrance, a warning.
Not Mozart, not Faure, Cherubini, Handel;
not even Beethoven, Verdi, Brahms;
not Britten with his poems by dead soldier-poet
Wilfred Owen incorporated into the Mass;
not Barber's Adagio for Strings, his memorial
for the dead of World War II made into a new
signature for war dead by Stone's *Platoon*;
not the Doors, *Apocalypse Now!*
No music at all, as in the image of battle-weary
soldiers emerging from their hiding places on
Hamburger Hill, silence more eloquent than
anything scored, ever; and here, besides these
images of death, a simple flower arrangement
between pictures, against a gallery wall:
white lilies in a vase and a small stack of business
cards that say "Viet Center Readjustment Counseling."

Young Girl with Two Kittens, a Chicken and Her Father's Rifle, Vietnam, 1974

She is dressed for an outing:
full skirt and printed blouse, all
their belongings crammed into
a few tightly packed boxes piled
for immediate transport way out
of town. Other, younger children
wait nearby, waiting for what happens
next, no one speaking, no one playing,
all eyes focused on the adults hurrying
about all around them, manic with
activity. Even the kittens cradled
beneath the girl's right arm are
transfixed, not squirming or protesting,
the chicken perched on their possessions
oblivious, above it all, all part of a freeze tag
game, the next move controlled by
someone who has no time for playing,
for releasing the children from their
trance. The rifle the child is guarding
should be an incongruous element in
this arrangement, but this is so clearly
a war zone where the only hope is
escape that it is all the details of domestic
life that are out of place, unnecessary,
soon to be of no use.

A Boy, a Dog and a Mortar

This is not the end of the earth
for war refugees; the end lies a few
miles down the mined highway
or in a ditch nearby, in an overturned
vehicle or in a sudden cross fire
between dissidents and government
troops or in a strafing run, carpet
bombing exercise, coordinates called in
by in-advance-of-a-mission scouts
or by nonexistent spook soldiers
on a run through the jungle to nowhere
using nonexistent frequencies, dead air,
to broadcast positions of another life;
this is not the end for a young boy
holding a malnourished dog to his chest,
the animal's discontent, resignation, no-use-
in-struggling look mirrored in the boy's
thousand-yard, staring-into-an-endless-
jungle look; the boy's downturned lips
signifying that another move means more
of the same, more loading onto troop
carrier trucks, just another illusion of
mobility and escape, the mortar propped
on the family's meager luggage the essential
component to taking the next giant step
toward what lies just beyond the end.

A Roadblock Marker along the Highway Outside Phnom Penh

Right of way is established near
Phnom Penh by unmistakable road
markers: a discarded, soiled right shoe,
the top half of a battered human skull,
a battle-scarred, rusted and bullet-holed
helmet and the barrel end of a no-longer-
serviceable small arms weapon pointing right.
A soldier taps the base of the skull
with a long white stick to see if it is mined
or perhaps he is moving the danger/
warning signs, playing a game of calculated
misdirection, assuming all portents along
the highways to hell that is Southeast Asia
circa 1973 are more real and reliable
than anywhere else, bushwhacking new trails
the enemy mines at night.

Combat Elephants in Vietnam

stand, as if posed, at jungle's edge,
fully armed North Vietnamese regulars
perched on their shoulders, smiling
for the camera, all thoughts of recent
encounters, successful ambush raids
momentarily forgotten, camouflaged
pith helmets set roguishly to one side,
an absurdist's parody of backlot
Rama of the Jungle movies in real life
as etched into the deepening furrows
of the elephant's faces, those deep-set,
unblinking eyes.

R. Capa's Last Rolls of Film

Imagine the men taken in rare early 50s
color film, those soldiers of misfortune
apprenticed to death, walking through
savannah grass, searching for their shadows,
ghosts;
imagine the sickle-like blades of an air cargo
plane between flights parked on buckling tarmac,
men watching the incoming, propellers of negative
skylight bringing with it the coming monsoon season,
rain;
imagine the mortally wounded man at photographer's
feet, limp extended fingers, bent joints, tripped
by a mine, a pure reaction shot, no time for framing,
a miracle of composition, the plainest of facts;
imagine what follows, another mine triggered,
fragments released, concussive blasts, more bodies
on a corrupted ground, the still-warm hand,
blank eyes inside an upside-down hourglass,
blood staining a spill of sand, a division
of fire ants on parade, everything after
fatally exposed.

Wandering in the Cage

for Sean Flynn and Dana Stone, m.i.a Cambodia

Captured high-riding red Honda bikes
at Charlie/Khmer checkpoint, assuming
they'd be released, detained for brief
interviews, interrogations; arrogant or
naïve or just plain crazy, no one knows.
They expected to return with the story
of a lifetime, tales to be told and embellished
over endless pipes of the local weed,
heavy shit, as noncombatants front-loaded
with cameras, more balls than brains, composing
shots for wire service release, cover articles
at *Life, Time, Paris Match,* finding instead
Year of the Monkey misfortune during
escalating hostilities, bomb-them-back-
to-the-Stone Age mentalities, no release
imminent, possibly friendly fire-wounded,
jungle-fevered, confined to bamboo cages
to be pissed on, tormented, prodded and poked,
regularly beaten as white demons, photo-
journaling hell from inside the Inferno.

The Girl in the Picture

The pain in her face
says it all, what went
wrong here, a peacekeeping
mission like a police action
gone straight to hell upside
down and crazy, over under
sideways down all at once
on a road leading away
from a torched village in
Vietnam, refugees fleeing.
Running, as she is running,
completely naked, nothing
else matters but the idea of
escape, trying to get out of
her skin, a burn of napalm
affixed to her back, her legs;
no running can ever erase
the pain, remove the wounds,
take the fire out once it
has been applied; once seen,
this image is imprinted forever,
has us running on that road
with her, calling out for the
madness to stop, as if it were all
a bad dream that could be
stopped by waking up.

Acknowledgments

Art Mag: "Mary Ellen Mark's American Odyssey," "My Dream Date with Sylvia Plath," "Ralph Steadman's Macbeth"
Big Scream: "Mary Ellen Mark's Ward 81"
Blue Collar Review: "Our Lady of Perpetual Longing"
Dead Snakes (reprinted online): "Kelly Flores with Casper the Friendly Ghost"
Glass Tesseract: "Combat Elephants in Vietnam"
Hollins Critic: "Raising the Dead, Requiem Exhibit"
Homestead Review: "A Boy, a Dog and a Mortar"
Kind of a Hurricane Press: "Mapplethorpe's Hand and Flower (2)"
Loch Raven Review (online): "Our Lady of the Kitchen Appliances"
Long Shot: "The Assassination of JFK in Alchemy," "Judith and the Head of Holofernes," "Winged Victory as Wagner Heroine in Minotaur," "After Viewing, Requiem," "The Flower Arrangement," "Dead Photographer's Exhibit," "R. Capa's Last Roll of Film"
Parting Gifts: "Halloween," "Mapplethorpe's Model," "Mapplethorpe's Hand and Flower (1)," "Ralph Steadman's Brain of Hunter S. Thompson According to Gray's Anatomy," "Beckett's Quadrant 1 & 2"
Pine Hills Review (online): "Mapplethorpe's Patti," "Ralph Steadman's Dmitri Shostakovich in Abbey," "Ralph Steadman's Milosevic in Mas Tequila," "My Dream Date with Diane Arbus"
Raven Chronicles: "Young Girl with Two Kittens"
Skidrow Penthouse: "Our Lady of the Striped Pajamas"
Slipstream: "'Teenagers,' Brighton Beach, Coney Island"
Sulphur River Review: "Girl in the Picture"

Cover artwork by Gene McCormick; author photo by Valerie Catlin; cover and interior book design by Diane Kistner; Warnock Pro text and titling

About FutureCycle Press

FutureCycle Press is dedicated to publishing lasting English-language poetry books, chapbooks, and anthologies in both print-on-demand and ebook formats. Founded in 2007 by long-time independent editor/publishers and partners Diane Kistner and Robert S. King, the press incorporated as a nonprofit in 2012. A number of our editors are distinguished poets and writers in their own right, and we have been actively involved in the small press movement going back to the early seventies.

The FutureCycle Poetry Book Prize and honorarium is awarded annually for the best full-length volume of poetry we publish in a calendar year. Introduced in 2013, our Good Works projects are anthologies devoted to issues of universal significance, with all proceeds donated to a related worthy cause. Our Selected Poems series highlights contemporary poets with a substantial body of work to their credit; with this series we strive to resurrect work that has had limited distribution and is now out of print.

We are dedicated to giving all of the authors we publish the care their work deserves, making our catalog of titles the most diverse and distinguished it can be, and paying forward any earnings to fund more great books.

We've learned a few things about independent publishing over the years. We've also evolved a unique, resilient publishing model that allows us to focus mainly on vetting and preserving for posterity the most books of exceptional quality without becoming overwhelmed with bookkeeping and mailing, fundraising activities, or taxing editorial and production "bubbles." To find out more about what we are doing, come see us at www.futurecycle.org.

The FutureCycle Poetry Book Prize

All full-length volumes of poetry published by FutureCycle Press in a given calendar year are considered for the annual FutureCycle Poetry Book Prize. This allows us to consider each submission on its own merits, outside of the context of a contest. Too, the judges see the finished book, which will have benefitted from the beautiful book design and strong editorial gloss we are famous for.

The book ranked the best in judging is announced as the prize-winner in the subsequent year. There is no fixed monetary award; instead, the winning poet receives an honorarium of 20% of the total net royalties from all poetry books and chapbooks the press sold online in the year the winning book was published. The winner is also accorded the honor of being on the panel of judges for the next year's competition; all judges receive copies of all contending books to keep for their personal library.

www.ingramcontent.com/pod-product-compliance
Lightning Source LLC
LaVergne TN
LVHW020938090426
835512LV00020B/3420